Russell Wilson

Phillip Rivers

Von Miller

Todd Gurley

Tom Brady

Larry Fitzgerald

RAIDERS

Khalil Mack

JJ Watt

George Kittle

Bobby Wagner

Odell Beckham

Ezekiel Elliott

Drew Brees

DeAndre Hopkins

Dak Prescott

Aaron Rodgers

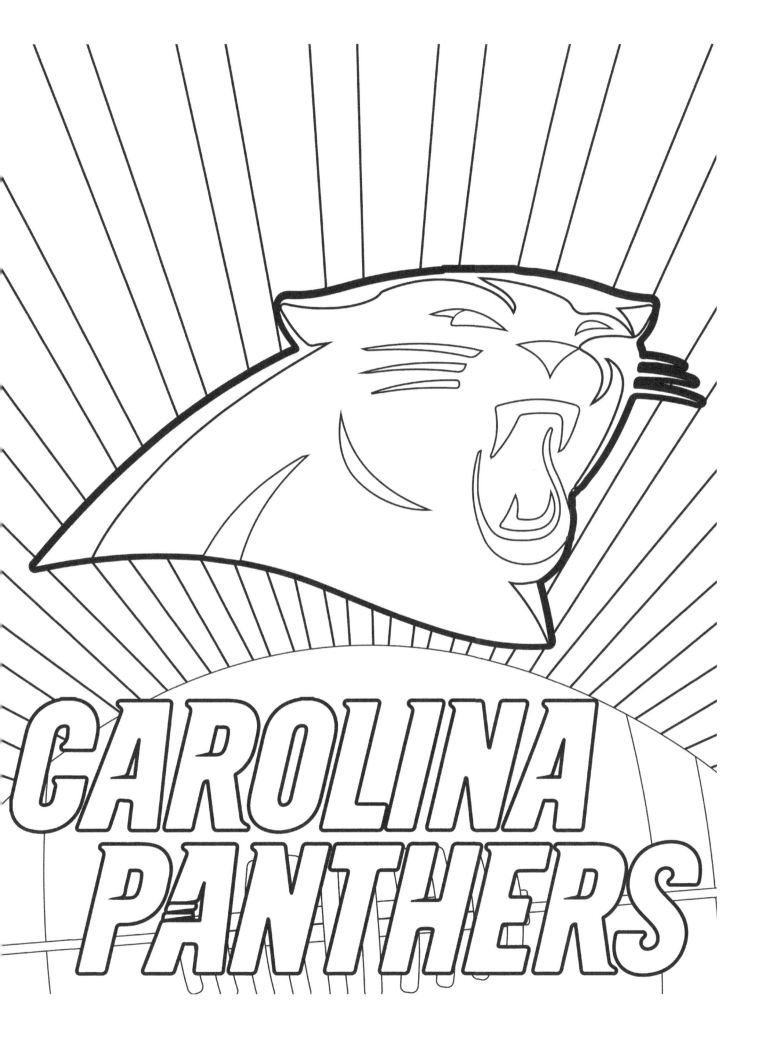

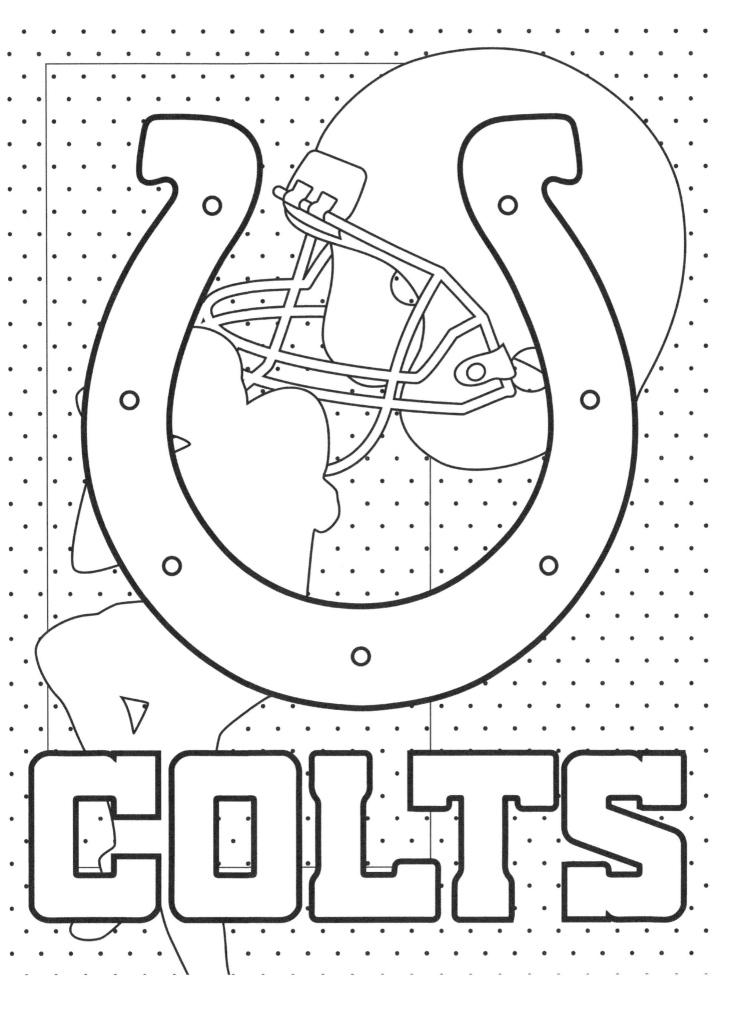

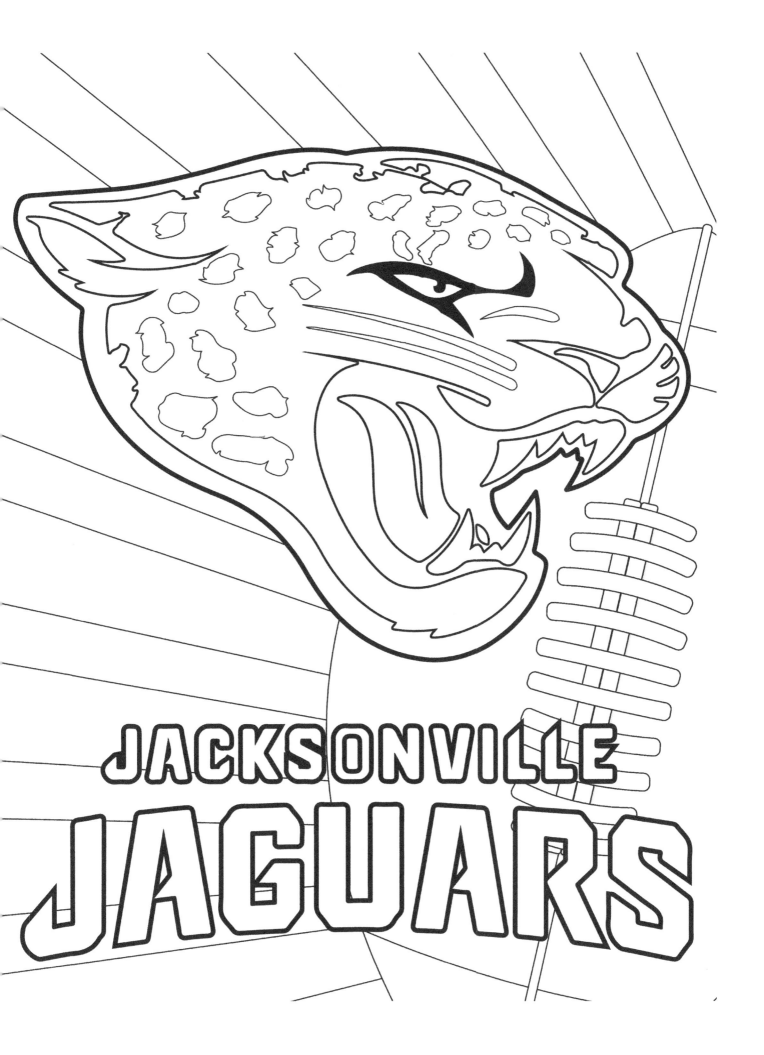

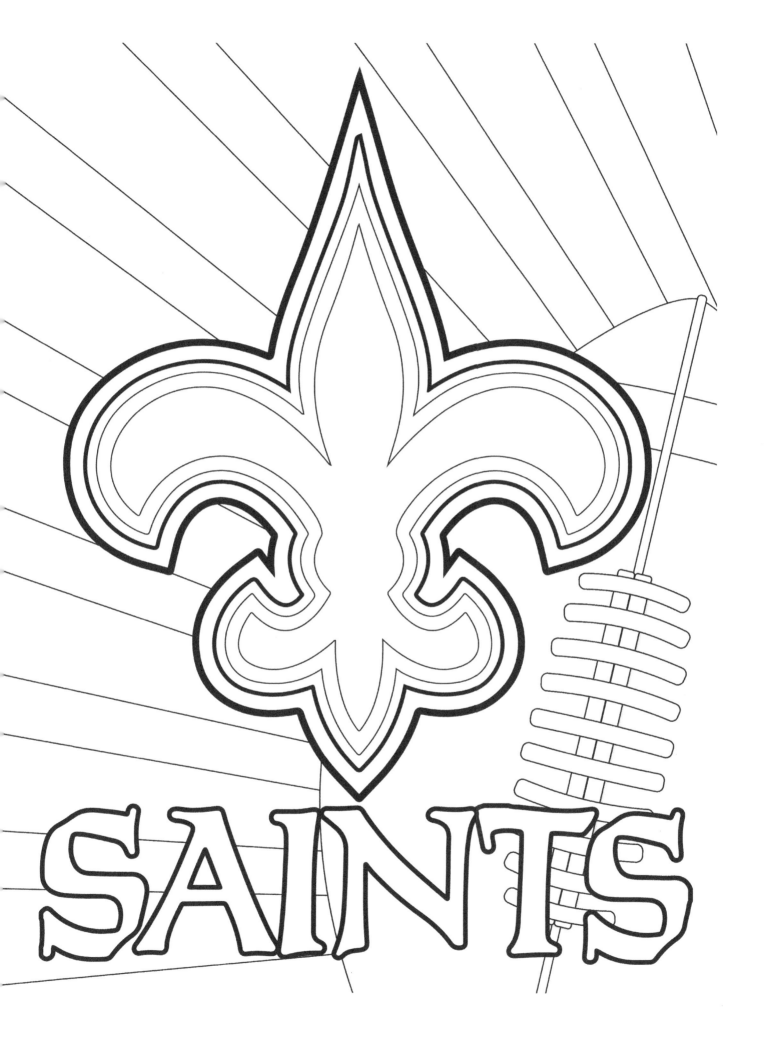

Made in the USA
Las Vegas, NV
23 April 2024

89038337R00066